MW00873031

100 +  Frequently Asked Interviev

Database Testing

By Bandana Ojha

## Introduction

"The book 100 + Frequently Asked Interview Q & A in Database Testing "contains database testing interview notes with simple and straightforward explanations. Rather than going through comprehensive, textbook-sized reference guides, this book contains only the information required for interview to start their career as database tester. It covers database testing, SQL queries ,sub queries, procedure, constrains, index, tables, table joins, DBMS,RDMS , data driven test, frontend testing, backend testing and many more.

Wishing good luck to all my readers!!!

Please check this out:

Our other best-selling books

500+ Java & J2EE Interview Questions & Answers-Java & J2EE Programming

200+ Frequently Asked Interview Questions & Answers in iOS Development

200 + Frequently Asked Interview Q & A in SQL , PL/SQL, Database Development & Administration

100+ Frequently Asked Interview Questions & Answers in Scala

100+ Frequently Asked Interview Q & A in Swift Programming

100+ Frequently Asked Interview Q & A in Python Programming

100+ Frequently Asked Interview Questions & Answers in Android Development

100+ most Frequently Asked Interview Questions & Answers in Manual Testing

Frequently asked Interview Q & A in Java programming

Frequently Asked Interview Questions & Answers in J2EE

Frequently asked Interview Q & A in Mobile Testing

Frequently asked Interview Q & A in Test Automation-Selenium Testing

**************************************************?

1. What do you understand by Database testing?

Database testing is the process of testing Data integrity, Data validity , Database performance, Functions, Procedure and Triggers.

2. What are the different types of Database Testing?

DB Testing can be categorized into 3 categories based on the functions and structure of a database.

Structural Database Testing

Functional Database Testing

Non-functional Database Testing

3. Why database testing is important?

In a database, data comes from multiple applications and there is a possibility that harmful or incorrect data is stored in the database. Database testing process ensures that the correct and unique data (without bug) delivers to the correct location. These bugs may cause some serious issues like; dead-locking, data corruption, poor performance, inconsistency, etc. Therefore, there is a need to check database components regularly. In addition, data integrity and consistency should be checked regularly.

To ease the complexity of calls to database backend, developers increase the use of View and Stored Procedures. These Stored procedures and Views contain critical tasks such as inserting customer details (name, contact information, etc.) and sales data. These tasks need to be tested at several levels.

Black box testing performed on front-end is important but makes it difficult to isolate the problem. Testing at the backend system increases the robustness of the data. That is why database testing is performed on back end system.

4. Explain the process of database testing.

The process to perform database testing is similar to testing of other applications. DB testing can be described with the following key processes –

Setting up the environment

Run a test

Check the test result

Validating according to the expected results

Report the findings to the respective stakeholders

5. What is data driven test?

Data Driven Testing(DDT) is an automation testing process where an application is tested with multiple test data. It is creation of test scripts where test data and/or output values are read from data files instead of using the same hard-coded values each time the test runs. This way, testers can test how the application handles various inputs effectively.

6. What are the types of data driven testing?

There are four types of data driven testing –

Dynamic test data submission through keyboard

Data Driven Tests via .txt, .doc flat files

Data Driven Tests via front-end objects

Data Driven Tests via excel sheet

7. How to test database manually?

Testing database manually involves verifying the data entered in the front end is available in the back end or not. The same verification process applies for delete, update, insert etc.

8. What are the common types of data backups?

There are two types of backup that can be used –

Physical Backups – Physical backup includes taking back up using 3rd party backup tools like Veritas net back, IBM Tivoli Manager or user manager backups using OS utilities.

Logical Backups – Logical backup of database includes taking back up of logical objects like tables, indexes, procedures, etc.

A common tool to take data backup is Oracle Recovery Manager (RMAN) that is an Oracle utility to take database backup.

9. How DB testing is different from Front-end testing?

DB testing involves testing of back-end components which are not visible to users. It includes database components and DBMS systems such as MySQL and Oracle.

Front-end testing involves checking functionalities of an application and its components like forms, graphs, menus, reports, etc. These components are created using front-end development tools like VB.net, C#, Delphi, etc.

10. What is a Database?

A database is a collection of information in an organized form for faster and better access, storage and manipulation. It can also be defined as a collection of tables, schema, views and other database objects.

11. What is structural database testing?

When database structure is tested that involve tables, schema, function, database server and triggers, then it is called testing of the database structure.

It involves validation of all elements/object, which is primarily used for data storage and are not directly exposed to end user.

## 12. What is non-functional testing?

Multiple testing is involved in multiple categories like security testing, stress testing, compatibility testing, load testing, and usability testing. All of these types of testing are known as non-functional testing.

## 13. What is functional database testing?

The functional database testing involves the requirement of specifications which are needs for user transaction as input or output.

It involves null values handle, length of a column, a data type of column. It will also check the derived output tables or column should be available. All the field name should follow the standard naming convention as per business requirement.

## 14. How do you test load/stress testing?

Need to check load or stress test by processing a large set of data in minimum time. It will check the system response; load testing is done. If the load exceeds the user's process it is known as load/stress testing. Examples of load/stress testing are downloading the set of data, executing multiple applications on a single computer.

## 15. What are the steps to test data loading?

Following steps need to follow to test data loading

Source data should be known

Target data should be known

Compatibility of source and target should be checked

In SQL Enterprise manager, run the DTS package after opening the corresponding DTS package

You have to compare the columns of target and data source

Number of rows of target and source should be checked

After updating data in the source, check whether the changes appear in the target or not.

Check NULLs and junk characters

16. What is performance testing and the bottlenecks of it?

Performance testing is a software testing technique to determine that how a system performance in terms of speed, sensitivity, and stability under a heavy workload.

The performance testing requires expensive tools and well-trained and experienced testers for operation.

17. What are the challenges come while performing database testing?

Some of the challenges are below:

Scope of the testing is large

Scaled down test database

Changes in database structure

Complex test plans

Good understanding of SQL

18. Name a few tools that are used by a tester to generate test data for a database system.

The following tools are used to generate test data –

Data Factory

DTM Data Generator

Turbo Data

19.What are the common types of data backups?

There are two types of backup that can be used –

Physical Backups – Physical backup includes taking back up using 3rd party backup tools like Veritas net back, IBM Tivoli Manager or user manager backups using OS utilities.

Logical Backups – Logical backup of database includes taking back up of logical objects like tables, indexes, procedures, etc.

20.Name a tool to take data backups?

A common tool to take data backup is Oracle Recovery Manager (RMAN) that is an Oracle utility to take database backup.

21.Name the common actions performed in Database recovery testing?

The following actions are performed in database recovery testing –

Testing of database system

Testing of the SQL files

Testing of partial files

Testing of data backup

Testing of Backup tool

Testing log backups

22.What do you understand by database security testing?

Database security testing is performed to find the loop holes in security mechanisms and also about finding the vulnerabilities or weaknesses of database system.

23.Name a few objectives of Database security testing.

Database security testing is performed to check the following aspects –

Authentication

Authorization

Confidentiality

Availability

Integrity

Resilience

24. What all things are required for writing good test cases in database testing?

Knowledge of following things is required before writing the database test cases:

First, understand the application completely and functional requirement of the application.

Second, check-out other entities that have been used in an application; back-end database tables, joins between the tables, cursors (if any), triggers (if any), stored procedures (if any), input parameter and output parameters for developing that requirement.

After collecting all necessary information, write down the test case with different input values for examining all the resources.

Writing test cases for back end testing is opposite to functional testing, one should use the white box testing technique.

25. What is retesting & how it is different from data driven testing?

After execution of the test in terms of finding the defect that has been already detected and fixed. Re-execution of the same test with different input values to confirm the original defect has been successfully removed is called Re-testing .Retesting is a manual testing process whereas application testing done with entire new set of data. Data Driven Testing is an automation testing process where an application will be tested with multiple test data. It is simple and easy than retesting where tester just sits in front of the system and enter different new input values manually from front-end interface, it is really boring technique.

26. What are various types of SQL statements?

SQL or structured query language has the following types of statements:

Data Manipulation Language or DML

Data Control Language or DCL

Data Definition Language or DDL

27. What is Table testing?

Table testing involves the testing of table and column names. Here front-end columns are mapped, while back-end names may remain the same. Data-type and size of the column must remain the same and as per the business requirement and should be mapped to front-end application. Here, in this testing, constraint testing is also required that may include testing of the foreign key, primary key and other conditions related to table or data. In table testing, cluster or non-cluster table indexing is also being tested.

28. What is  Trigger testing?

For this testing, rules are the same for the procedure and function testing. Here it has been checked that whether the trigger is being executed as per specific event requirement or on the occurrence of a particular event or not.

29. What is Database Server testing?

Here database server configuration is being checked. Execution processing capacity, storage capacity, and RAM should be as per user requirement.

30. What is schema testing?

The schema testing is being done in the way so that the name of frontend and backend schemas should be matched. The checkpoints involved in this testing are the validation of schema format, as sometimes the requirement of schema structure may differ from the requirement of the business process and the front-end application structure. Here, unmapped tables, columns, and views are also get verified.

31. How are database test cases being written?

After getting functional requirements, the user must understand table structure, Joins, Cursors, Stored procedure, parameters, and triggers. Then you can write a test-case along with different values as the inputs to these objects.

32. What is RDBMS?

RDBMS stands for Relational Database Management System. RDBMS is a database management system (DBMS) that is based on the relational model. Data from relational database can be accessed using Structured Query Language (SQL)

33. What is SQL testing?

SQL Test uses the open-source tSQLt framework, a set of T-SQL tables, views, stored procedures, and functions. SQL unit testing runs through simple queries which use the framework to check the values of your data types and to mock database objects.

## 34. What is Database Black Box Testing?

Database Black Box Testing involves

Data Mapping

Data stored and retrieved

Use of Black Box techniques such as Equivalence Partitioning and Boundary Value Analysis (BVA)

## 35. What do we need to check in Database Testing?

Generally, in Database Testing following thing is needed to be tested

Database Connectivity

Constraint Check

Required Application Field and its size

Data Retrieval and Processing with DML operations

Stored Procedures

Functional flow

## 36. What do you mean by query optimization?

Query optimization is a process in which database system compares different query strategies and select the query with the least cost.

## 37.How to check a trigger is fired or not, while doing database testing?

It can be verified by querying the common audit log where we can able to see the triggers fired.

38. What is Data migration and how does a tester test the Migration Data?

Data base Migration testing is done with the help of the Mapping document that defines the complete mapping from the source to the target and also the transformation logic that has to be applied while migrating the data from one DB to another. The Tester has to create SQL Queries with reference to the mapping document provided. There are few validations that would be followed while testing database migration like Data type, Length, Count, Duplicate, Null Value, Referential Integrity, Minus Query validations, Data Completeness etc.

39. What are the key points that should be considered while performing database recovery testing?

The following key points are to be considered while performing database recovery testing –

Time span when changes or modifications occurs in database system.

The period by which you want your recovery plan conducted.

The sensitivity of data in database system. More critical the data is, the more regularly you will need to test the software.

40. How do you test if your database is updated when data is entered in front-end application?

You can go to the database and run a relevant SQL query. In WinRunner, you can use database checkpoint function. If the application provides view function, then you can verify the same from the front-end.

41. How can stress testing be performed?

Here, the large amount of data is being tested for load in minimum time. The system response is being tested, when load testing is being done. In case if the load exceeds the user process, then it is known as load or stress testing. The testing examples may include multiple application execution on a single computer or downloading datasets.

42. What is load testing and give some examples of it?

To measure the system response, load testing is done. If the load exceeds the users pattern it is known as stress testing. Examples of load testing are downloading the set of large files, executing multiple applications on a single computer, subjecting a server to large number of e-mails and allotting many tasks to a printer one after another.

43. What steps does a tester take in testing Stored Procedures?

First the tester should to go through the requirement, as to why the particular stored procedure is written for. Then check whether all the required indexes, joins, updates, deletions are correct comparing with the tables mentions in the Stored Procedure.

44. How to test a DTS package created for data insert update and delete?

Data Integrity checks should be performed. IF the database schema is 3rd normal form, then that should be maintained.

45. What conditions are to be checked if the data is inserted, updated or deleted using a text file?

Check to see if any of the constraints have thrown an error. The most important command will have to be the DELETE command. That is where things can go really wrong.

Most of all, maintain a backup of the previous database.

46. How do SQL queries will affect the performance of the application?

Yes, sql queries make a lot of impact on the whole performance of application. A poorly written sql query by a developer can take long time to generate a report or retrieve data from data base. So, we need to take few precautions while writing queries, as a database tester I will also review the queries written by a developer. For example: get rid of nested sql queries as much as possible and make use of joins.

47. How can you retrieve unique rows from a table?

I can do that by using a DISTINCT keyword in my sql query. e.g.

 select DISTINCT * from books where book_category = 'science';

48. What is used to check data loading during database testing?

Query analyzer can be used to check data loading.

49. How to check a trigger is fired or not, while doing database testing?

It can be verified by querying the common audit log where we can able to see the triggers fired.

50. How to test data loading in Data base testing?

You have to do the following things while you are involving in Data Load testing.

You have known about source data (table(s), columns, datatypes and Constraints)

You have to know about Target data (table(s), columns, datatypes and Constraints)

You have to check the compatibility of Source and Target.

You have to Open corresponding DTS package in SQL Enterprise Manager and run the DTS package (If you are using SQL Server).

Then you should compare the column's data of Source and Target.

You have to check the number to rows of Source and Target.

Then you have to update the data in Source and see the change is reflecting in Target or not.

You have to check about junk character and NULLs.

51. What are the different stages involved in Database Testing

verify field level data in the database with respect to front-end transactions

verify the constraint (primary key,foreign key)

verify the performance of the procedures

verify the triggers (execution of triggers)

verify the transactions (begin,commit,rollback)

52. What is a DB trigger?

A DB trigger is a code or programs that automatically execute with response to some event on a table or view in a database. Triggers are created to enforce integrity rules in a database. A trigger is executed every time a data-modification operation occurs (i.e., insert, update or delete).

Triggers are executed automatically on occurrence of one of the data-modification operations.

53. What is the difference in execution of triggers and stored procedures?

-The main difference between database trigger and stored procedure is that the trigger is invoked implicitly, and stored procedure is invoked explicitly.

-Transaction Control statements, such as COMMIT, ROLLBACK, and SAVEPOINT, are not allowed within the body of a trigger; whereas, these statements can be included in a stored procedure.

54.What are the uses of triggers?

Basically, triggers are used to create consistencies, access restriction and implement securities to the database. Triggers are also used for –

Creating validation mechanisms involving searches in multiple tables

Creating logs to register the use of a table

Update other tables because of inclusion or changes in the current table.

55. What is DBMS?

A Database Management System (DBMS) is a program that controls creation, maintenance and use of a database. DBMS can be termed as File Manager that manages data in a database rather than saving it in file systems.

56. What is RDBMS?

RDBMS stands for Relational Database Management System. RDBMS store the data into the collection of tables, which is related by common fields between the columns of the table. It also provides relational operators to manipulate the data stored into the tables.

57.What is the difference between DBMS and RDBMS?

The primary difference between DBMS and RDBMS is, in RDBMS we have relations between the tables of the database. Whereas in DBMS there is no relation between the tables(data may even be stored in files).

RDBMS has primary keys and data is stored in tables. DBMS has no concept of primary keys with data stored in navigational or hierarchical form.

RDBMS defines integrity constraints to follow ACID properties. While DBMS doesn't follow ACID properties.

58. What is Database White Box Testing?

Database White Box Testing involves

Database Consistency and ACID properties

Database triggers and logical views

Decision Coverage, Condition Coverage, and Statement Coverage

Database Tables, Data Model, and Database Schema

Referential integrity rules

59. What is Database Black Box Testing?

Database Black Box Testing involves

Data Mapping

Data stored and retrieved

Use of Black Box techniques such as Equivalence Partitioning and Boundary Value Analysis (BVA)

60. What is the use of optimized load?

Optimized load is much faster and preferable especially for large set of data. It is possible if no transformation is made at the time of load and no filtering is done.

61. What is the difference between GUI Testing and Database Testing?

GUI testing is user interface testing or front-end testing

Database testing is back-end testing or data testing.

GUI testing deals with all the testable items that are open to the user to interaction such as Menus, Forms etc.

Database testing deals with all the testable items that are generally hidden from the user.

The tester who is performing GUI Testing doesn't need to know Structured Query Language

The tester who is performing Database Testing needs to know Structured Query Language

GUI testing includes invalidating the text boxes, check boxes, buttons, drop-downs, forms etc., majorly the look and feel of the overall application

62. What is Normalization?

Normalization is the process of organizing data to avoid duplication and redundancy.

63. What are the advantages of it?

 Some of the advantages are:

Better Database organization

More Tables with smaller rows

Efficient data access

Greater Flexibility for Queries

Quickly find the information

Easier to implement Security

Allows easy modification

Reduction of redundant and duplicate data

More Compact Database

Ensure Consistent data after modification

64.How many Normalization forms are there?

There are 5 forms of Normalization

First Normal Form (1NF): It removes all duplicate columns from the table. Creates table for related data and identifies unique column values

First Normal Form (2NF): Follows 1NF and creates and places data subsets in an individual table and defines relationship between tables using primary key

Third Normal Form (3NF): Follows 2NF and removes those columns which are not related through primary key

Fourth Normal Form (4NF): Follows 3NF and do not define multi-valued dependencies. 4NF also known as BCNF

65. What is De-normalization?

De-normalization is the process of attempting to optimize the performance of a database by adding redundant data.

66. Why De-normalization is necessary?

De-normalization is necessary because current DBMSs implement the relational model poorly. A true relational DBMS would allow for a fully normalized database at the logical level, while providing physical storage of data that is tuned for high performance. De-normalization is a technique to move from higher to lower normal forms of database modeling in order to speed up database access.

## 67. What is an Operator in SQL?

Operators are used to specify conditions in an SQL statement and to serve as conjunctions for multiple conditions in a statement.

## 68. How many types of operators are there in SQL?

Below are the sql operators

Arithmetic Operators

Comparison/Relational Operators

Logical Operators

Set Operators

Operators used to negate conditions

## 69. What is  Database query?

DB query is a code written in order to get the information back from the database. Query can be designed in such a way that it matched with our expectation of the result set. Simply, a question to the Database.

## 70. What is an SQL subquery?

SQL subquery is a means of querying two or more tables at the same time. The subquery itself is an SQL SELECT statement contained within the WHERE clause of another SQL SELECT statement and separated by being enclosed in parenthesis. Some subqueries have equivalent SQL join structures, but correlated subqueries cannot be duplicated by a join.

## 71. What is log Cache?

Log cache is a memory pool used to read and write the log pages. A set of cache pages are available in each log cache. The synchronization is reduced between log and data buffers by managing log cache separately from the buffer cache.

## 72. What is the difference between a temporary tablespace and a permanent tablespace?

A temporary tablespace is used for temporary objects such as sort structures while permanent tablespaces are used to store those objects meant to be used as the true objects of the database.

## 73. Which schema object instructs Oracle to connect to a remotely access an object of a database?

A database link (DBLink)is a schema object in one database that enables you to access objects on another database. The other database need not be an Oracle Database system. However, to access non-Oracle systems you must use Oracle Heterogeneous Services

## 74. What is SQL Injection threat?

SQL Injection threat is the most common type of attack in a database system where malicious SQL statements are inserted in database system and executed to get critical information from database system. This attack takes advantage of loopholes in implementation of user applications. To prevent this user inputs fields should be carefully handled.

## 75. What is @@ERROR?

The @@ERROR automatic variable returns the error code of the last Transact-SQL statement. If there were no error, @@ERROR returns zero. Because @@ERROR is reset after each Transact-SQL statement, it must be saved to a variable if it is needed to process it further after checking it.

76. What are the different types of locks in database?

The different types of locks in database are-

Shared locks – Allows data to be read-only(Select operations), prevents the data to be updated when in shared lock.

Update locks – Applied to resources that can be updated. There can be only one update lock on a data at a time.

Exclusive locks – Used to lock data being modified(INSERT, UPDATE, or DELETE) by one transaction thus ensuring that multiple updates cannot be made to the same resource at the same time.

Intent locks – A notification mechanism using which a transaction conveys that intends to acquire lock on data.

Schema locks- Used for operations when schema or structure of the database is required to be updated.

Bulk Update locks – Used in case of bulk operations when the TABLOCK hint is used.

77. How many types of Privileges are available in SQL?

There are two types of privileges used in SQL, such as

System Privilege: System privileges deal with an object of a particular type and specifies the right to perform one or more actions on it which include Admin allows a user to perform administrative tasks, ALTER ANY INDEX, ALTER ANY CACHE GROUP CREATE/ALTER/DELETE TABLE, CREATE/ALTER/DELETE VIEW etc.

Object Privilege: This allows to perform actions on an object or object of another user(s) viz. table, view, indexes etc. Some of the object privileges are EXECUTE, INSERT, UPDATE, DELETE, SELECT, FLUSH, LOAD, INDEX, REFERENCES etc.

78. Can there be multiple return statements within a function?

Yes, there can be multiple RETURN statements within a function though only one is executed. After the value is retuned, the control passes back to the calling environment and function processing is stopped.

79. What are the different types of data models ?

Following are the types of data models

      Entity relationship model

      Relational model

      Hierarchical model

      Network model

      Object oriented model

      Object relational model

80. What is Straight Table?

A straight table is much better at the time of sorting as compared to the pivot table as we can sort it according to any column as per our choice.

81. What are orphan records?

Orphan records are the records having foreign key to a parent record which doesn't exist or got deleted.

82. Is a null value same as that of zero or a blank space?

A null value is not at all same as that of zero or a blank space. NULL value represents a value which is unavailable, unknown, assigned or not applicable whereas a zero is a number and blank space is a character.

83. What is the difference between static and dynamic SQL?

Static SQL is hard-coded in a program when the programmer knows the statements to be executed.

Dynamic SQL the program must dynamically allocate memory to receive the query results.

84. What is indirect reference of schema objects?

When any procedure or function references another schema object through an intermediate procedure, function, or view, then the reference is called indirect reference.

85. Name few schema objects that can be created using PL/SQL?

Stored procedures and functions

Packages

Triggers

Cursors

86.How to test procedures and triggers of a database?

To test procedures and triggers of database, we need to have knowledge on input and output parameters. EXEC statement is helpful to run the procedure and examine the behavior of the tables.

Let's see how to test procedures and triggers of a database

Open database project in solution explorer

Go to view, Click on database schema

Open the project folder from the schema view menu

Right click on the object that has to be testing and click on the dialog box say Create Unit Tests

Create a new language test project

Choose to insert the unit test or create a new test and then click OK

Project that has to be configured will be done by clicking on the Project Configuration dialog box

Finally, configure the project and click on OK

## 87. What is data mining?

Data mining refers to using variety of techniques to identify nuggets of information or decision-making knowledge in bodies of data and extracting these in such a way that they can be put in the use in the areas such as decision support, predication, forecasting and estimation.

## 88. What is a mutating table?

A mutating table is a table, which is in the state of transition. In other words, it is a table, which is being updated at the time of triggering action. If the trigger code queries this table, then a mutating table error occurs, which causes the trigger to view the inconsistent data.

## 89. What is Self-Join?

Self-join is set to be query used to compare to itself. This is used to compare values in a column with other values in the same column in the same table. ALIAS ES can be used for the same table comparison.

## 90. What is Cross-Join?

Cross join defines as Cartesian product where number of rows in the first table multiplied by number of rows in the second table. If suppose, WHERE clause is used in cross join then the query will work like an INNER JOIN.

91. What is the difference between cross join and full outer join?

A cross join returns cartesian product of the two tables, so there is no condition or on clause as each row of table A is joined with each row of table B whereas a full outer join will join the two tables based on condition specified in the on clause and for the records not satisfying the condition null value is placed in the join result.

92. What is the difference between keep and joins?

Keep and joins do the same functions but in keep creates the two tables whereas join only creates the one table. Keep is used before the load or select statements.

93. What is a Relationship and what are they?

Relation or links are between entities that have something to do with each other. Relationships are defined as the connection between the tables in a database. There are various relationships, namely:

One to One Relationship.

One to Many Relationship.

Many to One Relationship.

Self-Referencing Relationship.

94. What do you mean by flat file database?

It is a database in which there are no programs or user access languages. It has no cross-file capabilities but is user-friendly and provides user-interface management.

95. What is relational algebra?

It is procedural query language. It consists of a set of operations that take one or two relations as input and produce a new relation.

## 96. What is specialization?

It is the process of defining a set of subclasses of an entity type where each subclass contains all the attributes and relationships of the parent entity and may have additional attributes and relationships which are specific to itself.

## 97. What are transaction control statements? Can they be used within the PL/SQL block?

Transaction Control statements are the COMMIT and REVOKE commands that control the logic of transactions within a database. These statements are valid within a PL/SQL block. The COMMIT command terminates the active transaction and makes the changes permanent to the database. The ROLLBACK command terminates the active transaction but cancels any changes that were made to the database.

## 98. What is the test scenario to test a database migrated from one sql server to another?

First of all, we need to check what all enhancements and changes happened to the SQL Server where we are planning to migrate.

Next, design the test case according to the following consideration:

Data type that has been used.

Length of the data field of SQL Server (Server into which we are migrating the data) should be same as the SQL Server from where we are taking out the data.

Each and every task should be organized correctly.

## 99. What is indexing and what are the different kinds of indexing?

Indexing is a technique for determining how quickly specific data can be found. It is used for query performance optimization. Indexing can be of the following types –

Binary search style indexing

B-Tree indexing

Inverted list indexing

Memory resident table

Table indexing

## 100. What are implicitly defined records?

Implicitly defined records are those that do not have the need to describe each field separately in the record definition. The structure of the record is not defined using the TYPE statement; instead, the %ROWTYPE attribute is used to define the implicit record to have the same structure as the database record.

## 101. What are indexes and mention different types of indexes?

Indexes are database objects and they are created on columns. To fetch data quickly they are frequently accessed. Different types of indexes are:

B-Tree index

Bitmap index

Clustered index

Covering index

Non-unique index

Unique index

102. What is the way of writing test cases for database testing?

Writing a testcases is like functional testing. First you have to know the functional requirement of the application. Then you have to decide the parameters for writing testcases like

Objective: Write the objective that you would like to test

Input method: Write the method of action or input you want to execute

Expected: how it should appear in the database

103. Can stand-alone programs be overloaded?

No, stand-alone programs cannot be overloaded; however, packaged sub-programs can be overloaded within the same package.

104. Can you invoke a stored function or procedure from the oracle forms in the database?

Yes, a stored procedure or function can be invoked from the Oracle Forms and the result can be used for further programming.

Interview Q & A series-9
200+
Interview Q & A in
iOS Development

Swift
Programming
By Bandana Ojha

Interview Q&A Series- 7
Frequently Asked
Interview Q & A
in Python Programming

By Bandana Ojha

Interview Q & A Series -15
Android
Development

Frequently Asked
Interview Q & A

Interview Q & A Series - 8
100+ Frequently asked
Interview Q & A in
Scala

Scala Programming
By Bandana Ojha

Interview Q & A series -11
100+ Frequently Asked
Interview Q & A

in Swift
Programming
Bandana Ojha

Interview Q & A Series-6
Frequently Asked
500+ Java & J2EE
Interview Q & A

J2EE
Java

Java JSP Servlet EJB JMS
JDBA JNDB
By Bandana Ojha

Interview Q & A Series-5
FREQUENTLY ASKED
INTERVIEW Q & A IN J2EE

JSP      EJB
SERVLET   JMS
JDBC    JNDB

By Bandana Ojha

Interview Q & A Series -4
Frequently asked
Interview Q& A in
Java

Java

By Bandana Ojha

Interview Q & A Series-13
100+ Frequnetly asked
interview Q & A in

Database
Testing

Interview Q&A Series-2
Frequently asked
Interview Q & A

Test Automation
Selenium Testing
By Bandana Ojha

Interview Q & A Series -3
Frequently Asked
Interview Q&A
in Mobile Testing

iOS
By Bandana Ojha

Interview Q & A Series -12
200+
Frequently asked
Interview
Q & A
in SQL
PL SQL
DATA BASE
Development & Administration

Bandana Ojha

Interview Q & A series -1
200+
Interview Q & A

in MANUAL
TESTING

90%Frequently
Asked Q & A

Interview Q & A Series - 14
100+ Interview Q & A
in
Angular JS

A

90% Frequently
Asked Q & A

Made in United States
Orlando, FL
31 December 2021

12703795R00021